Original title:
Briar Ballads

Copyright © 2025 Creative Arts Management OÜ
All rights reserved.

Author: Oliver Bennett
ISBN HARDBACK: 978-1-80566-743-8
ISBN PAPERBACK: 978-1-80566-872-5

Rhythms of the Twisted Wilds

In tangled woods where laughter grows,
A squirrel dons a tiny hose.
He waters plants with jest and cheer,
While neighbors call, 'He's quite austere!'

A raccoon winks as he pulls a prank,
Dives in treasure, steals a tank.
The birds all chirp, 'What's he up to?'
He hides their snacks, shall we pursue?

Old badger croons a silly tune,
Dancing under the chuckling moon.
His friends all giggle, stomp their feet,
A wild party, oh what a feat!

Through wild and weird, the critters roam,
In the funhouse woods they call their home.
With every twist, a chuckle grows,
Nature's jest, it overthrows!

Echoes of the Enchanted Thorns

In the midst of thickets, pranced a cat,
With a hat that was far too big for that.
It winked at the birds, who laughed in the trees,
And danced with the leaves in the playful breeze.

A hedgehog in slippers joined the parade,
Strutting about with a comical grade.
He slipped on a twig and fell on his back,
Then rolled down the hill with a shown-off knack.

The flowers all giggled, the mushrooms would sway,
As critters enjoyed their whimsical play.
A corncob pipe sang a jig to the night,
While shadows all tangled in faint starlight.

So raise up your glasses to mischief and cheer,
For laughter lives larger when friends are near.
In corners where giggles and thorns intertwine,
The echoes of joy in the moonlight do shine.

The Woven Tangle of Dreams

Oh, the dreams that are tangled in twilight's glow,
With a rabbit that tiptoes on socks made of snow.
He hops over puddles with grace like a knight,
Spinning tales of the charms found in magical night.

A squirrel in pajamas reads tales of delight,
Under branches adorned with the lantern's soft light.
He twirls with a feather, sings songs of the breeze,
While crickets compose symphonies deep in the leaves.

The owls wink knowingly at plays in the sky,
As mischief unfolds while the night draws nigh.
With all of their laughter, the starlings narrate,
In a tapestry woven with dreams that await.

So hush little dreamers, lie down in your nests,
For the whimsy of night will bring out all the best.
Within every tangle where nonsense abounds,
A world full of wonder and giggles resounds.

Dusk's Crescendo in the Underbrush

When evening descends with a flick of a hat,
And dance of the crickets begins where they're at.
A raccoon performs with a broom in his paw,
As fireflies flash in a marvelous awe.

The bushes are swirling with stories untold,
Of mischief and laughter and antics so bold.
With beetles in bowties and mice on the floor,
Tonight there's a party – come join, there's more!

The moon peeks with giggles, its light is a tease,
While shadows sway softly, just swaying with ease.
All creatures unite in a chorus so bright,
Celebrating the silliness found in the night.

So gather your friends as the dusk takes a spin,
For the underbrush dances with laughter within.
With each fleeting moment, joy never can hush,
In the heart of the forest, it's always a crush.

Ballad of the Silent Briar

In a glade where the thorns grow quiet at dusk,
Lived a creature quite bold, but a bit full of musk.
He wore quite a crown made of dandelion seed,
And strutted his stuff like a comical breed.

With whispers of laughter that rustled around,
He pranced through the brambles, making funny sounds.
A rabbit with sneakers joined in on the fun,
And twirled like a dancer, oh, wasn't it run?

They showed off their moves, all the bugs gave a cheer,
While frogs clapped their hands that had never known beer.
The thickets were jiving, in rhythms so free,
For laughter was plentiful, as joyous as can be.

So tip your wild hat to the antics at play,
For life in the thorns can be funny, hooray!
In the heart of the garden, where dreams spin and fly,
Reside joys that are silly, beneath every sky.

Poetic Journeys of the Hidden Ferns

In secret woods, the ferns do sway,
They giggle softly, come what may.
With floppy fronds, they dance and leap,
Their laughter echoes, in woods so deep.

With each rustle, a tale unfolds,
Of silly sprites and gems of gold.
A toadstool throne, a king's delight,
In leafy laughter, day turns to night.

They sip on dew, and toast the moon,
In froggy hats, to a funny tune.
Each wiggle, each waltz, a sight to see,
Oh, the joy of being ferns, so free!

So join the dance, and sway along,
To the whispers of the fern folk's song.
In hidden glens, where laughter thrives,
The journeys bloom, where nature dives.

Dances of the Forgotten Blooms

In meadows bold, the blooms do prance,
With petals bright, they take a chance.
A daisy dons a tiny hat,
While buttercups chase a playful cat.

They twirl and spin, in colors bright,
Telling tales of sunny nights.
The tulips giggle, the roses laugh,
A quirky crew on nature's path.

In the gentle breeze, they sway in time,
To melodies caught in the tree's old chime.
With every rustle, a secret shared,
Of vibrant dreams, unprepared.

So join the merry, the dance delight,
With blossoms bold, in purest light.
In forgotten glades, where humor grows,
Lies the truth of the blooms that pose.

Serenades of the Verdant Enigma

In thickets green, where shadows play,
The secrets whisper, come what may.
With every rustle, a chuckle near,
The leaves conspire, with mischief clear.

In tangled vines, the riddles weave,
Each twist and turn, oh, who would believe?
The ivy winks, the mossy stone,
In nature's jest, we're never alone.

They sing of gnomes who steal the scene,
And squirrels who hoard their winter cuisine.
With cunning plans and rhymes so sly,
They spin their tales, as time drifts by.

So listen close, to nature's tune,
In verdant corners, beneath the moon.
Where laughter sprouts in leafy threads,
The serenades of greens, where joy spreads.

Vibrations of the Thicket's Depth

In shadowed glades, the secrets hum,
A choir of leaves, a joyful strum.
With squirrels chattering in delight,
While owls roll eyes, oh what a sight!

The branches sway, with rhythm bold,
Tales of mischief, waiting to unfold.
A raccoon juggling acorns bright,
As the sun dips low, embracing night.

With warming glow, the fireflies dance,
A dazzling show, a nightly chance.
The trees share whispers, soft and sly,
In thicket's heart, where giggles lie.

So let us twirl, beneath the stars,
With nature's jokes and unseen sparrs.
In wildwood corners, where laughter steep,
The vibrations of life, in depths we keep.

Refrains of the Wild Greenery

In the woods where the critters play,
Squirrels tell jokes, brightening the day.
With acorns as props, they dance and prance,
While rabbits all cheer, caught in a trance.

A turtle raced by, oh what a sight,
Declaring he's fast, with all his might.
But a slug took the lead, slow and unbent,
Leaving the crowd in bewildered content.

When leaves tickle cheeks, laughter will soar,
As frogs croak their tunes, always wanting more.
The wind carries giggles through branches so wide,
Where whispers of jokes on the breezes ride.

Ballads of the Nature's Tapestry

The flowers gossip, their petals aflame,
Comparing their colors, who's winning the game?
Dandelions chuckle, full of delight,
"Look at my fluff! I'm a fluffy white knight!"

A caterpillar swaggers, with style so fine,
Claiming he's royal, like it's divine.
But wait for his time, he'll shed that old skin,
And flaunt butterfly wings, oh let the fun begin!

Whimsy Among the Wistful Thorns

In prickly patches where laughter blooms,
A porcupine jokes about his sharp plumes.
While roses roll eyes, feeling quite thorny,
They can't help but chuckle, it's just so corny!

A fox in a hat struts with flair and pizazz,
Dancing with badgers, and giving a jazz.
With snickers and snorts they sway to the beat,
Enjoying the humor of nature's own feat.

Rhapsody of the Unruly Grove

In tangled trees where the sunlight can't peek,
A wise old owl hoots humorous cheek.
"Why did the crow sit on the telephone wire?
To keep his friends close and the call a bit dire!"

The raccoons are plotting a festive night feast,
With loots of the garden, they're style at least.
Their laughter echoes, a mischievous sound,
In the heart of the grove, where joy can be found.

Poems from the Silken Thorns

In the garden of whispers, the roses complain,
Where thorns tell tales of a mischievous chain.
Bumblebees giggle as they chase after flies,
And petals wear glasses, to outsmart the sighs.

The violets play cards with the daisies in rows,
While sunflowers posture, with their big, goofy bows.
A cricket competes with the witty old snail,
As the butterflies flutter in colorful flail.

Master of laughter, the moon peeks to glare,
At the sprouting tomatoes, with their sweet, silly flair.
The vegetables join in, for a dance full of cheer,
While each sprout and seedling erupts into beer!

Rooted in humor, the buds start to sway,
A symphony formed from the earth's grand ballet.
With thorns as the jesters and blooms as the queens,
Life in the garden is silliness seen.

Secrets of the Enveloped Meadow

In a meadow so green, with secrets untold,
The grass whispers gossip while flowers unfold.
Ants plot a scheme to steal crumbs from the breeze,
As daisies wink slyly, oh, if you please!

The butterflies flit with a curious grace,
While squirrels wear hats, making quite the big case.
They chat about chatter and gossip galore,
Chasing each other, they tumble and snore.

The mushrooms gather for a wild, wacky feast,
With acorns as platters and laughter increased.
As sunlight dips low, the shadows join in,
Adding jokes to the tales of this whimsical din.

A cat in the meadow, sleek, striped, and bright,
Dreams of a chase under the starry night.
The tales intertwine in the glow of the glow,
In this enveloped magic, where laughter will flow.

Dances in the Woven Undergrowth

Sneaky ferns wiggle as the rabbits parade,
While ivy grows curious, of the fun being made.
The shadows are dancing, with the crickets' delight,
As fireflies twinkle in a soft, twinkly fright.

Down in the undergrowth, a party unfolds,
Where mushroom chandeliers gleam with bold golds.
The snails wear their shells like a fancy tuxedo,
While beetles perform in a grand little ghetto.

Grasshoppers leap with a hop and a twirl,
As the spiders spin webs, giving twinkling whirl.
The ants take to stage with their synchronized steps,
In a dance that befits all those cozy inepts.

At dusk, all the critters take bows with delight,
Underneath a sky of shimmering light.
In this wondrous place, where the funny will grow,
The underwood thrives as the laughter does flow.

Musings of the Tangleweed's Heart

Amidst tangled thoughts of the weeds' merry heart,
The flowers conspire to throw a grand chart.
Dandelions giggle as they float in the air,
While thistles poke fun with a prick and a flare.

In shadows, the brambles weave riddles of cheer,
Where critters convene for their daytime career.
With caterpillars chatting and dreaming of wings,
They plot the day's mischief, oh, the joy that it brings!

The heart of the tangle beats wild with escape,
For every bound moment, there's magic to shape.
With laughter erupting, the blooms join the song,
In this garden of whimsy, where nothing feels wrong.

So come spin with the weeds, let your worries depart,
In the glee of the tangle, there's joy at the heart.
A tangle of humor, in nature's embrace,
Where every small chuckle finds its perfect place.

Thorns of Echoed Whispers

In the garden, shadows play,
Where whispers dance, and secrets sway.
A thorny jest, a prickly laugh,
Nature's joke, a wild photograph.

The hedgehogs wear their spiky crowns,
While bees gossip in floral gowns.
Each petal hides a chuckle dear,
As the moon grins, drawing near.

Through tangled paths, we skip and twirl,
Chasing laughter 'neath a glowing pearl.
Tickling vines with gentle hands,
This delightful chaos stands.

A thistle sings, a daisy quips,
In nature's realm, the laughter dips.
So heed the whispers, join the fun,
For in this bunch, we're all as one.

The Nightshade's Lullaby

When twilight falls, the giggles rise,
As nightshade blooms with sparkling eyes.
The owls wink with a knowing glance,
While shadows lead a merry dance.

The moon's a trickster, shining bright,
Casting laughs in the still of night.
Each petal whispers tales astir,
Of hedgehog kings and squirrel fur.

Sleep tight, little ones, in the breeze,
Where nightshade hums amongst the trees.
Ticklish spiders weave their dreams,
In this funny world of moonlit beams.

The stars chuckle, their eyes aglow,
As crickets join the playful show.
In this lullaby, we're all entwined,
With every chuckle, peace we'll find.

Embracing Shadows in Bloom

In gardens sly, the shadows creep,
Where giggles rise and secrets sleep.
With petals bold and thorns that tease,
We dance around, hearts full of ease.

The daisies wink, in playful jest,
As shadows spin their nightly fest.
Each blossom wears a cheeky grin,
Inviting all to join within.

A gust of breeze, a chortle flies,
Where laughter blooms and reason dies.
In tangled greens, we weave our fables,
Creating tales on sunlit tables.

So wade through blooms, embrace the night,
With every shadow, find delight.
In this madcap realm, we shall play,
Through hilarious games, we'll find our way.

Secrets of the Tangled Vines

The vines entwine, a playful snare,
Holding secrets whispered in the air.
A playful twist, a cheeky leap,
They hide the giggles that they keep.

Where blossoms tease with colors bright,
And mischief swirls like day meets night.
Each tendril darts, a teasing hug,
Inviting all to join the rug.

In this leafy labyrinth, we roam,
Finding joy, a second home.
A beetle laughs, a butterfly sings,
As we uncover all that spring brings.

With every glance, we spot the fun,
In tapestry of sun and run.
So let us dance where shadows lay,
Finding laughter in every clay.

Chronicles of the Thorned Whimsy

In a garden lush and green,
Sat a squirrel with quite the scene.
He danced and twirled on thorny vines,
Claiming them as circus lines.

The roses laughed, their petals swayed,
As critters joined in the grand parade.
A hedgehog juggled acorns with flair,
While butterflies waltzed in the air.

The thorns cried out, 'We're not for show!'
But the laughter only seemed to grow.
They tickled toes and pricked the air,
Creating chaos without a care.

In the end, when the sun did set,
The thorny crew laughed without regret.
For in their hearts, they all did see,
That fun blooms wild, just wait and be.

Verses Beneath the Canopy

Underneath a leafy roof,
Danced a mouse with quite the hoof.
He twirled and spun on a twiggy stage,
While frogs croaked loud, impressing the sage.

A rabbit joined with a silly hop,
As the beetles played on a soda pop.
They sang of cheese and sweet delight,
While fireflies twinkled, lighting the night.

They giggled at the thorny plants,
Who swayed along with leafy chants.
The trees shook heads, in mock dismay,
While owls hooted, "Let's play all day!"

So beneath this leafy dome,
Animals made their jolly home.
For in the woods, where laughter's free,
Fun was the heart of their jubilee.

Echoing Amongst the Green Thicket

In thickets thick where giggles roam,
A raccoon found a cozy home.
He stole a hat from a nearby gnome,
And wore it proud, as if to comb.

The ladybugs, in tiny boots,
Joined in dance, delighting in roots.
They formed a line in a silly queue,
Trading stories, both old and new.

The thorns observed and shook with glee,
"A party here? Oh, let it be!"
With prickles sharp and laughter loud,
They gathered round, a happy crowd.

As the sun dipped low in the sky,
The woodland friends let out a sigh.
With hearts so light and spirits high,
They vowed to meet before goodbye.

Fables of the Vine-Kissed Earth

Along the path of tangled greens,
A chubby ferret shared his dreams.
He wished to fly on a grapevine swing,
While turtles laughed, claiming the ring.

The snapdragons joined with a fiery grin,
Awakening the laughter within.
With tales of woe from the prickled vines,
They made a scene that surely shines.

The sunflowers bowed and cheered aloud,
As the critters sang, feeling quite proud.
For mischief bloomed in the heart of the day,
Turning thorns into crowns for play.

At twilight's call, they danced in light,
Leaving behind a trail of delight.
In a world where laughter spun the tale,
Even thorns could not help but scale.

Lament of the Hidden Thicket

In a thicket so dense, I tried to peek,
A squirrel threw acorns, it made me shriek.
With branches that scratch and leaves that play,
I tiptoed back home, oh what a day!

The badger just chuckled, my plight so dire,
His burrow was cozy, mine held a fire.
He offered me snacks, I had my regrets,
Left my sandwich behind, it's all that I get!

I danced with the shadows, a firefly waltz,
But tripped on a twig, oh my, what a vault!
The thicket erupted in laughter, oh dear,
Now every tree knows my name, crystal clear!

So next time I venture, I'll dress with more care,
And pack a good lunch, in case of the rare.
For in hidden thickets where shenanigans thrive,
A jester's delight keeps the spirits alive!

Chants from the Glooming Glade

In the glade where the shadows twist and twine,
Mossy stones giggle, they're all doing fine.
The owls tell jokes, their laughter surreal,
While frogs croak a tune, it's a crazy reel!

A raccoon with flair claims he's king of the night,
While fireflies hover, giving soft light.
The crickets join in, they're the backup band,
With a tap of my feet, I take my stand!

But then I got snagged on a thorny old vine,
It tugged at my shoe, oh it crossed the line.
"Get out of my way!" I shouted in glee,
But the plants just chuckled, "You're silly, you see!"

So I sing with the glooms, a hilarious scene,
The glade keeps it lively, it always feels green.
Let's dance with the shadows, and laugh till we ache,
For the glooming glade's magic is never a fake!

A Rose Amongst the Brambles

Amongst prickly thorns, a rose stood so bold,
Claiming her space, quite the sight to behold.
She preened and she posed, with petals so bright,
While brambles grew jealous, oh what a sight!

"Why can't I be graceful?" a thornbush complained,\n"I'm prickly and rough, all my charm is drained."
But the rose just laughed, with a twinkle in eye,
"You bring all the character, don't even deny!"

A bee buzzed in, wearing a crown of gold,
"Here comes the royal, all delicate and cold."
But the rose winked back, with a mischievous glee,
"Just wait till he stings you, then we will see!"

So dances continued, in that brambly place,
With roses and thorns, not a moment of space.
In the chaos of blooms, a comical spree,
Life's quirks among brambles, forever carefree!

Serenade of the Thorned Path

On the path where I wandered, in a tangle of green,
A thicket of thorns hid the world so serene.
With each silly step, I stumbled and swayed,
While giggles erupted from the roots that stayed!

The path seemed to giggle, with every misstep,
As branches reached out just to give me a rep.
"Is this a dance?" I mused, with laughter so bright,
I marveled at nature's peculiar delight!

A hedgehog nearby, with a quizzical look,
Waved me a hello, "You're lost, like a book!"
We roasted some berries, a humor-filled feast,
In that moment of whimsy, I felt like the least.

So here's to the journey, with laughter in tow,
Through thorny adventures, we awkwardly go.
For the path's serenade, a silly embrace,
Where fun is the rule, and joy finds its place!

Retrospective Rhapsody of the Green Maze

In a tangled green where I did play,
A squirrel stole my hat, oh what a day!
I chased him through the leaves so bright,
Yet all I found was my own delight.

The paths are twisted, like a jester's grin,
I laughed so hard, I forgot to win.
Every turn a twist, a laugh or scream,
The maze turned out to be a silly dream.

With every step, a new mishap grows,
Tripped on a root, fell into a rose.
The flowers giggle, the trees all sway,
In this merry maze, I'll forever stay.

As twilight falls, the frogs declare,
A concert starts, with quite the flair.
With funny tunes from the moonlit skies,
I dance with shadows, oh how time flies!

Laments of the Gnarled Path

Along the gnarled path, a trip I made,
Found old Mr. Fox in a comical charade.
His whiskers twitched like a dancer's feet,
His playful prancing, quite the treat.

Each step I took, a funny twist,
Stubbed my toe, oh how I hissed!
A laugh from the trees, as I hopped about,
Turns out the route was a silly route.

A crow flew down, demanding a snack,
I offered my sandwich, and he pecked the pack.
He cawed with glee, what a noisy jest,
In this gnarled path, it's laughter that's best!

At the end I found a mossy seat,
With friends like these, life is a treat.
We shared our tales, both funny and grand,
On this twisted road, we make our stand.

Songs from the Overgrown Sanctuary

In a sanctuary lush, where laughter blooms,
A goat stood proud, amidst the glums.
He bleated a tune, a silly refrain,
That chased away all worries and pain.

The sun peeked through, in dappled light,
While dancing rabbits performed in sight.
They twirled and hopped, full of surprise,
With giggles echoing to the skies.

A picnic laid out with crumbs galore,
I took a bite, then dropped some more.
The critters gathered, what a hilarious sight,
As I tried to shoo them, but found delight.

At twilight's call, the fireflies gleam,
Twisting and turning, like a lively dream.
In this overgrown place, we sing away,
With laughter as bright as the end of the day.

Sketches of the Forgotten Glen

In a glen where whispers carve the air,
I drew a doodle, with flair and care.
But the wind took it, with a laugh so sly,
Chased my sketch into the sky!

Colors splashed on leaves so green,
A tangle of laughter, a silly scene.
A deer showed up, all proud and grand,
Mocking my art, with a cheeky stand.

The stones all chuckled, yes, they knew,
Each stroke I made was a point of view.
With nature's jesters, I'd found my way,
In the quiet glen, where giggles stay.

As night descends, the stars all wink,
With every twinkle, the shadows think.
In this forgotten space, full of grace,
Lies a feeling of fun, in quiet embrace.

Rhythms of the Forest's Embrace

In the woods where squirrels dance,
Frogs sing songs in a wild prance.
Trees twist in laughter, limbs all shake,
Mushrooms chuckle, make no mistake.

Breezes giggle through the leaves,
As rabbits share their silly thieves.
A hedgehog wears a tiny hat,
Sipping tea, quite fine and fat.

Nuts roll down with playful glee,
Acorns plotting mischief spree.
Nature's jesters all unite,
In the forest, hearts feel light.

So join the mirth beneath the sky,
Where even owls can't help but sigh.
For laughter rings in every space,
In the woods, there's endless grace.

The Thorned Path to Reverie

Upon the path where thorns reside,
Comes a hedgehog, full of pride.
He trips and tumbles, does a spin,
Shakes it off like he's made of tin.

A fox wears shoes that squeak with flair,
Dancing 'round with nary a care.
Under the brambles, the creatures cheer,
As laughter echoes, loud and clear.

A raccoon juggles shiny things,
While grumpy badger scowls and flings.
With each mishap, the forest roars,
Creating tales of endless scores.

In dreams where mischief takes the lead,
Each thorny step becomes a seed.
For every stumble brings delight,
In the thorns, there's joy in sight.

Ballads of the Gnarled Glens

In gnarled glens, the stories bloom,
With every twist, bypassing gloom.
A wise old tree croons tales so tall,
As shadows mimic, they sway and sprawl.

Crickets chirp a rhythmic tune,
While mice motorboats under the moon.
A flower giggles, bright and bold,
As bees hum secrets, never told.

A squirrel plays a tiny lute,
While owls hoot, they join the route.
Through tangled roots, the laughter streams,
In glens where truth entwines with dreams.

With every rustle, life unfolds,
The funny tales, forever told.
In nature's ballad, joy resides,
In the gnarled glens, all care hides.

Lamentations from the Forest's Edge

At the forest's edge, a frog does bemoan,
His buried treasure, a forgotten cone.
He croaks a sad but funny tune,
While a raccoon chuckles, chasing the moon.

The trees sway gently, shaking their heads,
As rabbits roll on their cozy beds.
With every sigh from the creeping vine,
A chipmunk beams, "Life's just divine!"

With drapes of ivy and dandelion fluff,
They grumble softly, but it's all in fun stuff.
For every lament, a hiccup's near,
In the forest's edge, where laughter's dear.

So come hear the stories, both odd and grand,
For every misfortune is carefully planned.
From sorrow blooms a bright smiley badge,
At the forest's edge, join the joyful entourage.

Melodies of the Feral Bloom

In the meadow, a pig in a hat,
Sings to the moon, oh what of that?
A cow joined in with a jig and a spin,
While the cat on the fence wore a grin.

The daisies danced, all in a row,
Tickling each toe of a sleepy crow.
A rabbit with glasses, reading a book,
Giggled at mischief, the sneaky brook.

Our fox with a flute played tunes of delight,
As fireflies twinkled, adorning the night.
The whole wild gang, in a chorus so sweet,
Made music that echoed, a jovial beat.

And as dawn broke, the laughter slowed,
They packed up their songs, their merry road.
With a wink and a hop, they all waved goodbye,
'Til next time we meet, in the brightening sky.

Tales Beneath the Twisted Boughs

Under the branches where shadows play,
A squirrel tells stories that lead us astray.
With a nut for a microphone, he spins a great yarn,
Of daring escapes from an overripe barn.

The owl hoots gossip, oh what a tease,
While raccoons sneak past with their pies and their keys.
A magpie, quite chatty, adds spice to the tale,
As the fox rolls his eyes at the newest detail.

The mice have a dance, it's a wild little show,
As the hedgehog starts judging, quite ready to go.
With thumbs up or down, they're rating the fun,
In the heart of the woods, with a laugh and a pun.

With voices so bright, they make shadows sway,
Under the boughs where the creatures will play.
The tales may be tall, but the joy is sincere,
In the laughter that ripples from ear to bright ear.

Nocturnes of the Hidden Glade

In the glade where the fireflies flit and flash,
A bear in pajamas went out for a splash.
He tripped on a root, did a tumble and roll,
And the giggles erupted in a cacophony whole.

A raccoon holds court with a bright, shiny shell,
While the frogs start a choir that sings very well.
The moonbeams, they dance through the leaves up above,
As the creatures all join in a symphony of love.

The owlets are hooting a curious tune,
As the fox strums a guitar that he found by the moon.
The hedgehog keeps time by tapping his feet,
To a rhythm that sends all the critters to sleep.

As dawn's light creeps in, they bow with a flair,
Each creature retreats with a swell of fresh air.
With dreams by the river and laughter in flight,\nThey'll meet in the glade for a encore tonight.

Harmonies from the Thorny Pathway

On the thorny pathway, the hedges all sway,
As a duck in a bowtie quacks out a play.
With a wink to a rabbit, who's dressed up so fine,
They put on a show for a chance at a dime.

The crickets compose, with their legs playing strings,
A band of loud gigglers, with laughter that rings.
A beetle bassoonist joins in with a tune,
As the badger brings snacks, under the light of the moon.

The wind starts to hum a familiar refrain,
While the toads wear their hats, getting ready for rain.
The fun never ends as the dancefloor ignites,
With twirls and with leaps in the soft glow of nights.

As they bow and they cheer, each creature takes flight,
With plans for the morrow, such sticky delight.
A patch of good fortune, where silliness grows,
In the heart of the thickets, where everyone glows.

Fables of the Wildflower Dream

In a meadow where daisies dance,
The bumblebee's got a sweet romance.
With a butterfly dressed in polka dots,
They twirl and giggle in sunlit spots.

A sunflower wears a silly hat,
Saying, 'Oh my, what of that cat?'
The rabbit jumps with quite the hop,
While the grasshopper plays the banjo pop.

Underneath a sky of cotton candy,
The ladybug sings, her voice quite dandy.
The frogs croak jokes with such delight,
Making even the fireflies giggle at night.

At dusk they all share a lemonade,
Telling tales of the fun they made.
In the wildflower dream, life's a blast,
With laughter and joy that's sure to last.

Chants of the Gnarled Roots

In the forest where the gnarled roots twist,
A squirrel claims, 'I can't resist!'
He tightrope walks on a fallen log,
While the owl hoots, 'Oh, what a frog!'

The raccoon's mask is a bit askew,
He offers a dance, 'Come join the crew!'
The trees chuckle with a creaky sound,
As the acorns roll and spin around.

A hedgehog whispers to a shy old toad,
'Life's a circus on this winding road!'
With twirls and flips, they both collide,
Creating chaos, oh what a ride!

As night falls, the moon begins to glow,
The critters gather for the nighttime show.
With jokes and jests in the forest's root,
Laughter echoes in nature's loot.

Rhymes of the Verdant Maze

In a maze where the green vines curl,
A snail dreams big, with one slow twirl.
He races a tortoise, both have their fun,
In a game where the slowest is number one.

With bushes whispering silly tunes,
The flowers giggle beneath the moons.
The hedges play hide and seek all day,
While the wind joins in with a breezy sway.

A chipmunk juggles with acorns ripe,
Singing a ditty that's full of hype.
The grass sings back with a soft caress,
Merging notes in a playful mess.

When twilight comes, the maze aglow,
Fireflies join in a sparkling show.
In rhymes of laughter, time takes flight,
As critters rejoice till the morning light.

Verses of the Whispering Woods

In the woods where whispers weave and flow,
A fox tells tales of the dancing crow.
The trees lean in to hear the fun,
As critters gather, one by one.

A possum strums on a wooden seat,
The music makes everyone tap their feet.
The beetles march in a civil line,
While the butterflies flutter, all divine.

The brook giggles, bubbling with laughter,
Echoing stories of happily ever after.
A squirrel cracks jokes, as nuts fly high,
The laughter lingers, it never runs dry.

Under the stars, a grand feast awaits,
Sharing treats from old nature's plates.
In the woods where whispers twine and twirl,
Every creature's a star in this goofy swirl.

Echoes of the Wild Rose

In the thicket where foul winds play,
A cat once danced, oh what a sway!
He twirled with bees and yelled in glee,
While mice laughed hard tucked up in a tree.

From petals soft like a rosy drum,
A fox joined in, his paws went thrum.
With wild tunes and a jolly cheer,
They pranced 'round till they shed a tear.

The squirrels joined in, no fear at all,
Chasing shadows as they'd trip and fall.
A party brewed beneath the moon,
With laughter echoing, a silly tune.

So raise a glass to the wild rose crew,
With honey laughter that stuck like glue.
In the thickets where nonsense reigns,
The silly echoes will always remain.

Serenade of the Bramble Path

Upon the bramble path they meet,
A turtle donned a fancy seat.
"Now listen close!" he shouted loud,
"I'm the king of the wandering crowd!"

While hedgehogs rolled in a concert fine,
With tiny hats and snacks of brine.
A snail flailed wildly trying to sing,
Yet all that buzz just made hearts cling.

The brambles shook with laughter's clang,
As critters cheered, the woodland sang.
A merry jig in the bramble bower,
Each spin and swish gave nature power.

So gather 'round for the bounteous jest,
In shrub-throned glory, they're surely blessed.
With jokes and tales of the critter dance,
Join in the fun, take the chance!

Lullabies of the Enchanted Thicket

In the enchanted thicket, tigers swirl,
While owls hoot loud, and night-time twirl.
A bat wears glasses, reading a tome,
He shrieks of mysteries where fairies roam.

With crickets strumming on blades of grass,
And fireflies flicker like stars that pass.
A hedgehog croons a silly refrain,
Most of the notes kind of sound the same.

Lullabies echo, a twisted delight,
As frogs jump up in a moonlit fight.
Each twinkling star seems to giggle and sway,
As night unveils its whimsical play.

So cuddle close to the thicket's embrace,
Let laughter and dreams take you to a place.
Where funny creatures hum tunes in the night,
And all is jolly beneath the starlight.

Shadows of the Winding Vines

In shadows deep where the vines entwine,
A lizard struts in a suit so fine.
He tips his hat and winks with glee,
"Today, dear friends, please dine with me!"

With beetles buzzing, they set the stage,
Unrolling tricks page by page.
A dance-off sparks in the leafy halls,
Where laughter bursts and mischief calls.

The slugs parade, all gooey and grand,
While daisies sway, holding hands on stand.
Each twirl and spin, oh what a fuss,
With tiny critters causing a rush!

So in shadows where silliness shines,
Join party antics, and sip on the wines.
For in this merriment of leafy beds,
The winding vines turn giggles to threads.

Echoing Tales from the Verdant Maze

In a forest full of laughter,
A fox wore shoes much too tight,
He danced and tripped, oh what a clatter,
Squeaking shoes brought pure delight.

The owl hooted, 'What a sight!'
A turtle laughed from the bog,
'Next time wear sandals, it's polite,'
But the fox just shrugged with a smog.

A hedgehog joined with a grin,
He boogie-woogied with flair,
They spun and twirled, it was a win,
Till he prickled a squirrel with care.

So they sang through the leafy night,
With hiccups and snickers sublime,
In the maze where all felt just right,
Joined in joy, lost track of time.

The Luminescent Thorns' Reverie

At dusk, the thorns began to glow,
They chuckled softly, a gentle tease,
A firefly swooped low and slow,
'Who tucked you in with such ease?'

A rabbit hopped in a hurry,
With a wiggle, a jump, and a spin,
'Can't chat! I'm late, so don't worry,'
Off he dashed with a cheeky grin.

The thorns giggled back in glee,
'Oh, come back and frolic a while!'
But off he went, too fast to see,
The whims of night made him smile.

When morning came, they dimmed their light,
Adventures tucked in a leafy bed,
With tales of mischief and delight,
The thorns whispered dreams in their head.

Whispers of the Thorned Hollow

In hollow woods, where whispers dwell,
A crow found a hat, oh so grand,
He wore it high, it fit him well,
Pretending to be a mighty band.

He cawed and strutted with a flair,
'Look at me, I'm king of the scene!'
But slipped on a berry, oh what a scare,
Fell flat, still felt quite the queen.

A rabbit chuckled from the brush,
Said, 'Your royal crown is a jest!'
The crow replied with a jovial hush,
'This hat holds laughter, I'm the best!'

In every thorn, a giggle lay,
With tales of mishaps, bright and bold,
In the hollow where friends play,
Every moment is a story told.

Songs in the Twisted Grove

In the grove where the twisty trees,
Sang a song only squirrels could hear,
A raccoon joined with raucous ease,
    Belting tunes of good cheer.

With a caper and a clumsy twirl,
He bumped into the old oak's side,
The tree creaked back with a wobbly whirl,
    'Careful now, don't take a slide!'

The laughter echoed, the fun grew bright,
As critters danced on tangled roots,
Their giggles spun into the night,
With rhythm found in wild disputes.

So gather close, all who roam,
In the grove, where humor thrives,
With leafy laughter, we find our home,
Where silly times keep joy alive.

Reveries in the Overgrown Fields

In the fields where the weeds dance,
A cow took a spin, what a chance!
She twirled with delight, by a tree with a grin,
While a goat laughed aloud, fueling the din.

A rabbit on roller skates bounces about,
While squirrels throw acorns, with laughter, they shout.
A fox in a hat, tipped low on his brow,
Catches flies in the sun, what a curious plow!

A prancing young hen leads a conga line,
While the rooster sings tunes that are simply divine.
The wind whispers secrets, tickling the grass,
As frogs in tuxedos all gather to pass.

The blooms giggle softly, a symphony bright,
While dandelions puff dreams into the night.
In this quirky fair, with each spin and twirl,
Who knew that a field could dance and unfurl!

Notes from the Secreted Glens

In a grove where the shadows like to prance,
A hedgehog in spectacles leads a fine dance.
With a wink and a nod, he twirls with great flair,
While fireflies twinkle, like jewels in the air.

The mushrooms all chuckle, so round and so stout,
Telling tales of their capes, while the owls all pout.
A haiku contest begins with a splash,
As the brook gurgles laughter, a bubbly brash.

A raccoon in pajamas holds court on a log,
Conspiring with turtles, and one friendly frog.
They plot a grand feast, with berries and cream,
While boasting of mischief, each wild, silly dream.

In this hidden retreat, where laughter can soar,
The whispers of nature invite us for more.
Through petals and branches, the giggles flow free,
In the heart of the glen, what a sight to see!

Sutras of the Verdant Wonderland

In a meadow of jests, where the daisies unfold,
A snail, in a race, gathers stories retold.
While crickets compose melodies in the air,
A turtle with swagger shows off his fine wear.

Beneath the tall oaks, a picnic's in swing,
With ants as the waiters, delighting in bling.
The cake is a muffin, so grand and so fluffy,
And punny old beetles feel cheerful and huffy.

A parade of snails wears bright hats with flair,
While ladybugs gossip, and twirl without care.
Each bloom holds a secret, a giggle to share,
In this wondrous expanse, all worries lay bare.

As the sun dips below, painting skies with a smile,
The frogs sing their songs, making a whimsical pile.
In this land of delight, where silliness reigns,
The sound of pure laughter forever remains!

Harmonies in the Dappled Light

Under branches that sway in a breezy ballet,
A bear in a tutu goes prancing away.
With a wink and a roar, he leads an odd crew,
Of hedgehogs and bunnies, in a delightful view.

The sunlight spills gold on a sly little fox,
Who wears shoes from leaves, crafted right from the blocks.
He tap dances bravely, while squirrels throw shade,
At the pie-baking contest, with berries displayed.

A chicken declares she has found the best prize,
An acorn-shaped snack with a sprinkle of guise.
The frogs form a band, toasting marshmallows grand,
With dreams of tomorrow all close at hand.

As shadows grow long, the laughter grows bright,
In this forest of mirth, everything feels right.
Each twirl and each giggle, like music in flight,
Is the joy of the wild in the dappled light!

Stanzas of the Mysterious Briars

In the tangled vines where secrets lie,
A squirrel wore a tie, oh my!
He danced with glee, a dapper chap,
While birds watched on, there came a clap.

The bumblebees sang in hasty tune,
As hedgehogs grooved beneath the moon.
With shoes of thorns, they took a chance,
And rooted weeds joined in the dance.

A hedgehog asked a fox for flair,
"Can you teach me how to pair?"
The fox just laughed, with eyes agleam,
"Just roll with it, and live the dream!"

In this patch where laughter twines,
Nature's pranks are pure designs.
With every twist, a joke unfolds,
In brambles, joy is what we hold.

Lyrical Tales of the Untamed Land

In fields so bright, where daisies play,
A pig in boots leads the way.
He snorts a tune with utmost cheer,
As rabbits hop and drink their beer.

A hill of ants formed quite a band,
With tiny drums, they took a stand.
While crickets chirped a lively beat,
The owls just shook their heads in heat.

A fox appeared, with stories tall,
"You won't believe, I caught a ball!"
But it turned out to be a hat,
And none believed him, just sat flat.

Oh, the laughter in this merry patch,
Where critters meet and tales dispatch.
Together in this wild domain,
Life's a jest, a joyous gain.

Reflections in the Bramble's Embrace

A raccoon peeked from leafy veil,
Holding a fish, just like a tale.
He posed for pics, all smug and bright,
While frogs croaked jokes to share the night.

Deer danced lightly, a waltz so sweet,
With flowers joining on their feet.
A rabbit tripped, but said, "No fear!"
And hopped right back with hearty cheer.

In bramble bushes, tales unwind,
Of goofy pals, both sweet and blind.
With every laugh shared through the night,
The moonbeams twinkled, pure delight.

So in this thicket, wild and grand,
Nature's comedy takes a stand.
Each critter plays a prank or two,
In the bramble's arms, laughter's true.

Songs of the Secreted Petals

With petals soft and colors bright,
A bee performed its sweetest flight.
It hums a tune that's naught but glee,
As ladybugs buzzed, "Join the spree!"

Amidst the blooms, a peacock preens,
While ants debate on quilted seams.
A hat of flowers, quite the sight,
Has Mr. Toad looking just right.

The tulips spark a gossip train,
While daisies snicker, wild and vain.
In this garden, mirth shall reign,
For every joke, there's joy to gain.

So sing along, you flowers fair,
Let laughter dance upon the air.
In petals shy, secrets regale,
Together we sing, with hearty hail!

Reflections Among Twilight Thorns

In the garden where the shadows creep,
The roses gossip, their secrets to keep.
A squirrel in a top hat, what a sight to see,
Dancing with a jaybird, wild and free.

With twinkling stars above their heads,
They sing about the farmer's beds.
Each thorn a dancer, each petal a clown,
Under the moonlight, spinning around.

The hedgehogs chuckle, they can't get close,
To two silly rabbits who brag the most.
In this thorny realm of tutus and jest,
The laughter echoes, it's simply the best.

The night's a stage, the thorns the lights,
With every giggle, the humor ignites.
In twilight's embrace, let mirth be our guide,
Where roses waltz and mischief resides.

Echoes of the Hidden Bower

In the cozy nook where the sunshine peeks,
A frog in a crown says, "Just one more week!"
With daisies nodding as they join in the game,
The bower's alive, never quite the same.

A fox in a cloak tells stories of old,
Of beanstalks and giants, and treasures of gold.
The mice in the pantry are planning a feast,
With crumbs and with giggles, they rally the least.

The trees start to sway as the wind begins to hum,
Even the shy shy-shrooms join in the fun!
They chuckle and dance, each creature a friend,
In this secret arena, the joy has no end.

With whispers of mischief and laughter galore,
The echoes of fun keep on calling for more.
In a hidden bower where mirth finds a home,
Let's celebrate life, in hearts we will roam.

Fables from the Roots

Deep in the soil where the stories start,
The potatoes gather, swapping tales with heart.
"Remember the time we grew a bit shy?"
Said the carrot, while sipping a dew drop pie.

A turnip chimed in, with a wink and a grin,
"Let's not forget how we taught those weeds sin!"
The radishes giggled, turning a bright hue,
In the patch of delight, where the laughter grew.

The ants brought the news, they're planning a show,
Where veggies dance proudly, all aglow.
They polished their leaves, dressed up in a flair,
With chard as the diva, and peas as the pair.

Each tale a delight from the roots up above,
These fables remind us of friendship and love.
In this garden of whimsy and unruly cheer,
Let's spread joy through laughter, year after year.

Requiem for the Wandering Breeze

Oh, breezy sojourner, with mischief on wing,
You tickle the flowers, and make the birds sing.
You sneak through the meadows, a playful wight,
Whispering secrets to stars at night.

A leaf spins through laughter, a dance on the air,
The daisies all giggle as you tousle their hair.
With fluttering whispers, you jest and you play,
Guiding the clouds as they drift their own way.

In the fields of green grasses, you gamble with time,
Chasing the sunlight, you make everything rhyme.
"Watch out for rain!" the daisies declare,
But you twirl with a chuckle, without any care.

So here's to your journey, oh breeze of delight,
With every soft chuckle, you brighten our night.
In the requiem sung from the thicket and tree,
May laughter and joy always follow thee.

Hushed Murmurs of the Thorns

In the garden, gossip flows,
Thorns whisper secrets nobody knows.
Bumblebees buzz with tips so grand,
While roses chuckle, a blooming band.

A dandelion prances, full of glee,
Waving at clouds, so carefree.
Petals dance, a silly parade,
In this place where humor's made.

A hedgehog joins, sporting a hat,
Juggling berries, imagine that!
Laughter echoes through leafy halls,
While sunflowers stand tall, flipping their shawls.

What mischief waits where shadows play,
In the thorns where humor lays?
As laughter entwines with vines entwined,
The garden's charm, hilariously designed.

Twilight's Embrace in the Garden

When evening falls and shadows creep,
The flowers prepare for a fun night's leap.
Crickets tune their tiny fiddles,
While moonlight giggles, a grand-time riddle.

Fireflies don their sparkling gear,
Dancing in swirls, instilling cheer.
The ferns whisper jokes to the willow trees,
As laughter bounces on the evening breeze.

A raccoon pirouettes, all odds defied,
Searching for snacks with mischief wide.
Above, a bat dives, quick as a dart,
While daisies snicker, "Oh dear, so smart!"

In twilight's arms, the laughter sticks,
As nature plays its funny tricks.
Every shadow a giggle, every light a grin,
In this garden, where joy is spun.

The Melody of Twisted Roots

Roots entwined in a dance so odd,
They twist and twirl, giving laughter a nod.
A mushroom jigs to the quirky beat,
While snails applaud with tiny feet.

A squirrel scampers, juggling acorns bright,
Claiming, "Look, I'm a circus delight!"
While the wise old tree chuckles with pride,
At the silliness flourishing far and wide.

A rainbow worm sings a tune so spry,
Promising treats from the blueberry pie.
As grasshoppers hop with a rhythm so fine,
In this humble realm where nature does shine.

The roots play music, cheeky and loud,
With laughter reigning, oh so proud.
Every twist and bend a reason to cheer,
In a world where funny creatures endear.

Harpstrings of the Darkened Grove

In the grove where shadows bloom,
A harpist plays amidst the gloom.
The notes tumble down like raindrops bright,
Stirrings of laughter dance in the night.

A fox in tuxedo, slick as can be,
Takes center stage for all to see.
With juggling tricks and sly little plots,
He steals the show, tying silly knots.

The owls hoot in hilarious tones,
As they drum along with their bony bones.
Bats swing low, creating a scene,
In this darkened grove, where whimsy's queen.

Mirth weaves through the twisted trees,
Dispelling sorrow with a teasing breeze.
In shadows deep, where laughter flows,
The harpstrings play, and joy brightly glows.

Chiming of the Wicked Reeds

In the glade where whispers play,
The reeds engage in a cheeky fray.
They giggle and sway in the breeze's song,
While mischievous crickets chirp along.

A frog takes a leap, wearing a crown,
Declaring himself the king of the town.
But the reeds just laugh at his royal parade,
As they rustle in glee at the plans he made.

Veils of Stardust in the Thicket

Under the stars, the thicket's a show,
Where fireflies wink and secrets flow.
A raccoon spins tales with a sly little grin,
Of treasures discovered and places he's been.

He juggles ripe berries, oh what a sight!
While the owls hoot softly, joining the night.
With veils made of stardust, the laughter's so free,
As critters unite for a grand jubilee.

The Secret Symphony of the Brambles

In the heart of the brambles, a band starts to play,
With a hedgehog on drums and a mouse who'll sway.
The tune's quite absurd, a delightful charade,
As the bushes all dance with the music they made.

A rabbit comes in on a trumpet so bold,
With a flourish of hops, oh, watch the fun unfold!
The harmony's zany, a quirky delight,
Laughter erupts in the moon's silver light.

Harmony Amidst the Prickly Shadows

In shadows where prickle and fun intertwine,
A slow-witted tortoise sings out a line.
His friends giggle softly, they can't help but tease,
As he narrates tales of grandiose ease.

A quick-witted fox join in with a dance,
Flipping and flopping, he takes a chance.
The laughter grows loud, a symphony found,
In prickly shadows where joy abounds.

Whispers Between the Bramble Boughs

In a thicket where giggles grow,
The bushes plot a playful show.
With twigs that tickle passersby,
They laugh as wanderers wonder why.

A squirrel dons a tiny hat,
While hedgehogs dance, imagine that!
The thorns wear crowns of royal jest,
A comedy where nature's best.

Each bramble hums a cheeky tune,
As bees play cards beneath the moon.
The wind joins in with a soft sigh,
In this tangled world where chuckles fly.

So come, dear friend, the show won't wait,
In this wild wood, it's simply fate.
A lullaby of laughter sings,
Among the prickles, joy it brings.

The Enigma of the Spined Grove

In a grove where spines make art,
The puzzles start to play their part.
A porcupine with a pencil drawn,
Sketches riddles till the dawn.

With brambles forming perfect knots,
And bushes brewing silly thoughts,
A curious owl wears glasses wide,
Solving mysteries while he glides.

The winds are stumped, they blow askew,
Tickled by leaves in a twisty cue.
The silence bursts, a giggle flows,
In the spined grove where mischief grows.

So ponder here, if you dare roam,
Join in laughter far from home.
For every thorn's a funny twist,
In this enchanted, prickly mist.

Shadows Dancing on the Soft Ferns

Under ferns, the shadows play,
Beneath soft leaves, they wiggle, sway.
With mischief hidden in each fold,
They tell tales, in whispers bold.

A rabbit's laugh can fill the air,
As dance partners spin without a care.
The moon peeks in with a twinkling eye,
At shadows that leap and flicker by.

Fern fronds wave like hands in cheer,
Inviting all, come gather near!
With every twist, a giggle blooms,
In the shadows where laughter looms.

So join the frolic, let joy unfold,
In this world where shadows are bold.
With each soft rustle, fun is found,
Among the ferns, laughs abound.

Wandering Through the Prickled Song

Through thorny paths where melodies swell,
Each prick leads to a story to tell.
A thistle hums a catchy tune,
While crickets dance beneath the moon.

With every step, a chuckle slips,
As bushes tease with playful quips.
A hedgehog jives upon the scene,
In a concert of pricks, so keen.

The thorns applaud with gentle rustles,
While flowers laugh in joyful hustles.
Don't take a step too soon, my friend,
Or you may find a laugh that bends!

So wander on through this silly place,
Embrace the prickle, join the chase.
With every note, a grin will grow,
In this sprightly song, let laughter flow.

Stanzas of the Whispering Petals

Amidst the blooms, a tale unfolds,
Of gossiping petals, secrets told.
They chuckle softly in the breeze,
Tickling the bumblebees with ease.

A daisy winks at the clumsy fly,
Says, "You buzz, but oh my, oh my!"
The rose rolls her eyes with a dramatic flair,
"Be careful, you might fly right through the air!"

Lilies dance in their elegant gowns,
While the violets gossip 'bout the garden clowns.
Laughter erupts from the tulip crowd,
As the wind chimes in, humming loud!

With petals in tow, they twirl and sway,
Spreading cheer through the sunny day.
In the garden of whimsy, joy takes flight,
As blossoms share mirth from morning till night.

Chronicles Written in the Wild Air

In a world where daisies run free,
A buttercup challenges a buzzing bee.
"You think you're smart with that zippy flight?"
"Try blooming like me, oh what a sight!"

The trees lean closer, straining to hear,
As giggles ripple, loud and clear.
Squirrels toss acorns, what a brave show,
Declaring a challenge to the winds that blow.

Dandelions puff like fluffy clouds,
Racing the shadows, laughing loud.
Each petal's a story, swirling in air,
Nature's own comic, entered with flair!

A wise old oak rolls its leafy eyes,
Watching the antics beneath sunny skies.
With every gust, another tale's spun,
In the wild air, mischief is never done.

Rhapsodies of Nature's Cathedrals

In a grand hall of leaves and light,
Nature sings with all her might.
Mushrooms bow in the morning sun,
While dandelions groove and run.

The chipmunks chatter, setting the beat,
As the grasshoppers dance with little feet.
A symphony of chirps fills the air,
Conducted by breezes without a care.

Oh, the laughter of crickets fills the night,
As fireflies twinkle, shining bright.
A chorus of frogs joins in with a croak,
Creating a serenade from every oak.

As petals flutter, harmonies blend,
In the cathedrals where wonders transcend.
Nature's repertoire, never a bore,
Where every moment brings laughter galore!

Lament of the Shrouded Blossoms

Under a shroud of fog they sigh,
The shyest blooms, tucked up high.
"Why must we linger in shadow's hold?"
They bumble and mumble, feeling quite bold.

A forget-me-not pipes up, wise and spry,
"Don't fret, my friends, the sun is nigh!"
As a butterfly flutters, looking for cheer,
"Come out, my lovely blooms, have no fear!"

Poppies peek through, colors aglow,
"Why hide when the world has so much to show?"
The shy ones whisper, "We're waiting in vain,
Hoping the sunlight will ease our disdain."

But when beams break through, laughter erupts,
As every bloom bursts, happy and chucked.
No longer shrouded, they dance in delight,
In the morning sun, a heartwarming sight!

Triads of the Unseen Blossoms

In hidden nooks, the flowers grin,
They tickle bees with blooms of sin.
A windy jest, a playful sway,
They dance around in bright display.

With petals bright, they wear their charms,
They giggle at surrounding farms.
A honey bee, a clumsy fool,
A fuzzy dance, their lively school.

In sunlit fields, they steal the show,
With every breeze, their laughter flows.
Their silly ways, a fragrant spree,
You can't help but smile with glee.

So wander here on paths untold,
Where blooms of laughter unfold.
In this sweet world, so light and free,
Nature's comedy waits for thee.

Parables of the Mossy Cradle

In the cradle of the mossy ground,
Tiny creatures cavort around.
A hedgehog snorts, a snail slips by,
While crickets laugh and moths just fly.

A tale unraveled beneath the trees,
Where squirrels chatter with gentle ease.
They race along on branches high,
Each leap a giggle, oh my, oh my!

Under the dappled sunlit spot,
A wise old toad shares all he's got.
With tales of love and tales of woe,
His croaks a chorus, a charming show.

So nestle close to nature's riddle,
In this soft patch, where laughter's middle.
Each mossy laugh, each tiny cheer,
Brings joy abundant, bright and dear.

Chords of Nature's Whisper

The whispers tell of frolic and fun,
Where leaves twirl 'round like they've won.
A playful breeze, a tickling song,
Nature's orchestra, all day long.

The flowers sway, they hum and twang,
While butterflies dance to nature's clang.
Each chord a giggle, every note a spree,
A symphony inside the tall oak tree.

The ants parade with tiny drums,
Creating rhythms that make you hum.
With every step, they march in time,
Nature's jesters, a joyous rhyme.

So lend an ear to nature's play,
In every rustle, there's laughter today.
With chords that echo, light and bright,
The whispers of joy will take flight.

Vignettes from the Thorny Since

In a bramble patch, where thorns reside,
Grows a band of mischief, oh what a ride!
With poky poses, they smile with glee,
    Thousand prickles, a merry spree.

A caterpillar in a thorny stew,
Wiggles along, seeking its view.
"Oh, what a seat!" it grins and chats,
"Life's quite good, even with spats!"

But crows overhead start to squawk,
"Hey little critters, come take a walk!"
Down below, the thorns conspire,
"Let's prank the birds!" they sing with fire.

In this wild tangle, laughter's near,
With every twist, each tiny cheer.
So join the fun, let hearts commence,
In the quirky world of thorny sense.

Elegies of the Prickled Grove

In a grove where thorns do jest,
The prickle plants wear crowns of zest.
They throw a party, but oh, what mess!
Inviting bugs and a ruffled dress.

The caterpillars dance, oh so sly,
Twisting their wings, they leap and fly.
The roses giggle, with no reason why,
As bees buzz by, just to say hi.

Frogs croak tunes that are quite absurd,
While crickets chirp in a whispered word.
A dandelion's wish is blurted and blurred,
As the comical weeds are never deterred.

So raise a glass to the thorns and fun,
In this prickled realm, where laughter's spun.
With every poke, they delight, not shun,
For life's a riot, and they've just begun.

Anthems of the Elusive Bloom

In the garden, blooms play hide and seek,
Petals laughing, with colors so chic.
One peekaboo, then a cheeky tweak,
Whispering secrets, silent and meek.

Sunflowers chuckle as they follow the sun,
While tulips gossip, and have loads of fun.
Each blossom sways, a dance just begun,
While bees don tuxedos for the grand run.

A wily vine climbs high up the wall,
Hitching a ride on a ladybug's crawl.
With giggles and wiggles, they answer the call,
As nature's own jesters, they enthrall us all.

So sing out loud for the blooms so bright,
In gardens where laughter takes joyous flight.
Their antlered jokes bring day into night,
An elusive party, a wondrous sight.

Chronicles of the Verdant Shadows

In the shadows where the ferns do sway,
A troupe of frogs puts on a play.
With silly hats and a grand ol' display,
They croak the plot in a bumpy way.

Vines tangle up in a wild ballet,
Twisting and turning, they're led astray.
But laughter erupts; it's a comical fray,
As the wise old owl hoots, 'Come what may!'

Bumblebees buzz with a rhythm so bold,
Their tiny feet tap to stories retold.
The midnight blooms unveil yellow and gold,
As giggles and whispers in shadows unfold.

So sit in the greens, let the laughter seep,
In verdant shadows, where secrets keep.
With every twist, they sow fun so deep,
For nature's own humor is ours to reap.

Sagas of the Twisted Flora

In a patch of twists and twirls so bright,
The flora convene for a comical fight.
With funny facades that bring sheer delight,
Each petal a prankster, oh what a sight!

Thorns clutch their sides in exaggerated glee,
As daisies toss daisies in animated spree.
While the willow weeps, sipping tea with a bee,
Their chatter erupts, spreading wild jubilee.

Cacti tell tales with their prickly quips,
While ivies entwine with their sly little nips.
The sunflowers sway, full of laughter and flips,
In this twisted mischief, each plant tightly grips.

So gather 'round, let the flowers regale,
Of squishy tomatoes and a snickering snail.
In the saga of greens, where giggles prevail,
Nature's own jesters will never grow pale.

www.ingramcontent.com/pod-product-compliance
Lightning Source LLC
Chambersburg PA
CBHW070751220426
43209CB00083B/449